BLEACHERS IN THE SUN

Y York

BROADWAY PLAY PUBLISHING INC
New York
www.broadwayplaypublishing.com
info@broadwayplaypublishing.com

BLEACHERS IN THE SUN
© Copyright 2010 by Y York

First printing: November 2010
Second printing: September 2014
I S B N: 978-0-88145-436-9

Book design: Marie Donovan
Typographic controls: Adobe InDesign
Typeface: Palatino
Printed and bound in the U S A

ABOUT THE AUTHOR

Y's other third millennium plays include: EGGS;
...AND L A IS BURNING; GETTING NEAR TO BABY;
FRAMED, RIVER RAT AND CAT; NOTHING IS
THE SAME; FORK IN THE ROAD; THE FORGIVING
HARVEST; MASK OF THE UNICORN WARRIOR;
OTHELLO (4-character hip hop adaptation); KRISIT;
THE NEW DARK CLARITY; LUCINDA AND THE
WILD SWANS; DON'T TELL ME I CAN'T FLY;
and WOOF. Earlier work is happily still produced
in theaters across the country and is available from
Broadway Play Publishing Inc, Dramatic Publishing,
Saint Martin's Press, and Smith and Kraus. In
December, 2008, Y received the Smith Prize. She is the
recipient of the Charlotte B Chorpenning Award from
A A T E for her body of work and in 2006 received
the Hawai`i State Award for Literature. Y is a proud
alumna of New Dramatists, member of the Dramatists
Guild, Pen, and still lives with Mark Lutwak to whom
all things are still dedicated.

BLEACHERS IN THE SUN premiered at the ARTS at Mark's Garage, Honolulu, Hawaii, in April 2008, presented by Smashbox Productions (Tony Pisculli, Producer). The cast and creative contributors were:

TILLY ....Monica K C Coldwell
ZOE .... Jessica Haworth
JUDY ....Stephanie Kong
ROSE.. Kathy Hunter

Director.. Mark Lutwak
Set design ....Meleanna Aluli Meyer
Costume design ....Kathe James
Lighting design ....Bulldog
Sound & music .... Mark Lutwak
Stage manager... Squire Coldwell
Assistant director.. Nilva Panimdim

CHARACTERS & SETTING

Four eleven year-old girls; the actors are adults.

TILLY, *overweight, wants to be loved anyway*
ZOE, *claustrophobic, genius, hanging on to childhood*
ROSE, *newly rich, insecure, and suspicious of everything*
JUDY, *a cunning beauty with no money and little hope*

Fall, 2003

A NOTE ON PERFORMING THE PLAY

We have seen adults play children over the years. We know what works, and what reads phony and annoying. Perky doesn't work, jaunty hands on hips doesn't work, high funny voices don't work, "na na na *na* na" doesn't work. What makes an adult actor believable in a child role is emotional availability: being able to blush on cue, to allow inner guilt to rise to the surface without moving a muscle. It's understanding the power of stillness, lack of inhibition, the economy of motion, and, most importantly, how the subtext constantly percolates beneath the language. All the action is in the subtext. An adult actor committing to the subtext will find herself playing a child's actions.

And one must remember—these children are a very specific age: eleven. They are not small children; they are as intelligent as any adult. They lack only worldly experience and emotional knowledge. However, they are not yet adolescents. It is tempting to give over to "teen-speak". These characters are not yet of that age. They are aware of that world, and variously long to enter it, but they are still learning the moves.

When Tilly says, "Shit! Shit shit shit!" she is first of all speaking the epithet aloud for the first time in her life. The second through fourth times she speaks the word is both practice and liberation as she achieves another milestone.

There is meanness in the text: it doesn't require volume or violence. The words do plenty of harm on their own. Each character has her own "plight", but at no time engages in self-pity.

An anti-sentimental approach allows the text to be funny; and laughter makes the ultimate punch of the play stronger.

As of this writing, we are both still alive and happy to answer any questions that you may wish to pose through the publisher. Don't hesitate to ask.

Y York & Mark Lutwak

Now the frozen gambler he was very bored trying to create a next World War, he found a promoter who nearly fell off the floor, he said I never engaged in this kind of thing before, but yes, I think it can be very easily done. We'll just put some bleachers out in the sun and have it on Highway 61.

Bob Dylan, *Highway 61 Revisited*

for
Zoe, Olivia, Althea, Max, Charlotte, Sylvie, and Avery
my once and future eleven-year-olds

ACT ONE

Scene 1

(Behind the bleachers of a school track, TILLY *appears, looks around. She takes out a cigarette and fake smokes it; saunters around as if talking with other cool smokers. Unseen,* ZOE *comes around the bleachers.)*

TILLY: "Hey, got a light? *(Fake drags on cigarette)* Oh, a couple of years...I tried to quit but I'm addicted too much—"

ZOE: What's that supposed to be?

TILLY: Jeez, man, Jeez. *(She stuffs the cigarette in her pants pocket.)*

ZOE: Is that your mother's?

TILLY: It's mine.

ZOE: She'll kill you if she catches you, Tilly.

TILLY: She isn't going to catch me.

ZOE: Are you here to smoke? Is this where people smoke?

TILLY: Don't you have to meet your guy?

ZOE: I have fourteen minutes.

TILLY: Well, I have zero minutes.

ZOE: What's that mean?

TILLY: It means I want you to leave.

ZOE: Why?!

TILLY: I told you I hadda do something.

ZOE: Yes, but you didn't say I'd have to not be there.

TILLY: *(Adamant)* You have to not be there.

ZOE: ...You know, Tilly, some day, Friday, probably, there's going to be *another* quiz, and *somebody* is going to want me to sit way back in my seat so that she can see my answers again.

TILLY: I didn't look at your answers.

ZOE: "Two X plus X plus four equals thirteen. Solve for X."

TILLY: Five.

ZOE: Three.

TILLY: Okay, maybe you helped me out with an answer or two—

ZOE: Twenty.

TILLY: Sometimes you look at my paper, too.

ZOE: Just to make sure you write it down right.

TILLY: I know how to copy!

ZOE: Yes, you get a lot of practice.

TILLY: *(Growing impatience)* Okay...I'll make it up to you—but later.

ZOE: Thirteen more minutes.

TILLY: If you're staying, I'm leaving.

(TILLY fake stomps off. ZOE stays put.)

TILLY: What are you doing?

ZOE: Staying. I like it here. *(Investigating)* Quiet. Secret. *(Re under the bleachers)* Good cover. This is really good cover.

TILLY: Oh, come on, Zoe, don't start—

ZOE: Much better than the basement. The building can fall down on top of you in the basement, and then you're trapped.... Even if the bleachers collapse, you could find your way out.

TILLY: They don't bomb schools.

ZOE: Not yet.

TILLY: Not ever. Not for a hundred years. We bombed them back to the stone age. Boosh!

ZOE: You know what the worst part is?

TILLY: You not going away.

ZOE: The worst part is not if you get killed. The worst part is when you get trapped and stuck all alone in your room with a thousand pounds of rocks on top of it.

TILLY: That doesn't sound so worst to me.

ZOE: *(Panic)* Alive and trapped in the dark is terribly worst.

TILLY: If I was stuck in my room, I'd eat my cookies which would make it not "terribly worst"!

ZOE: No, no see, you *can't* eat your cookies—

TILLY: For once, nobody tattling.

ZOE: You can't eat them because you can't *find* them. Dark, like the darkest night. No light can get in. All the little children are trapped under the rubble—

TILLY: They were office towers—no children—

ZOE: All in the dark, terrified of the darkness—

TILLY: No—see— *(Lighting a match from her pocket)* You don't have to be in the dark, Zoe. You can light a match.

ZOE: Open their little eyes and, instead of light, see black nothingness—

TILLY: Look, look at this! Matches, so I'm never in the dark. Here. Take them, and you'll never be in the dark.

(ZOE *takes them.*)

TILLY: Keep them with you in your pocket forever. No darkness.

(*The matches relieve* ZOE *of her fears.*)

ZOE: Thanks. Hey, what are you doing with matches? You better not light that cigarette.

TILLY: I don't have matches—I just gave them to you!

ZOE: (*Russian accent*) "Tank you, Natasha. I so glad to get matches. Now, never in darkness!"

TILLY: Zoe, can't you *please* just go— (*Checks to see if anybody is coming.*)

ZOE: (*Russian accent continues until noted.*) "I not Zoe. I Yelena from Russia."

TILLY: Nobody cares about the Russians anymore.

ZOE: "Yes, *now* say that, but soon Natasha will change tune, will care plenty about Russians, will want Yelena around for all time."

TILLY: Why? Why am I going to want "Yelena" around for all time?

ZOE: "Because soon Yelena get big big bucks. Buy many greasy fast food items for Natasha. Father of Yelena say we get great big house and pony and Yelena take all friends to Disneyland."

TILLY: Who is it *this* time? Who died and left you a million dollars *this* time?

ZOE: "Old Auntie die. She leave me bundle."

TILLY: (*Pointedly*) Is your old auntie who died like your old uncle who died?

ZOE: "No. Auntie more rich. Yelena heiress."

TILLY: There was no uncle. You're not an heiress.

ZOE: "Not yet, but soon, soon, get big inheritance."

TILLY: *(Testing)* When is the funeral?

ZOE: "...Was last week."

TILLY: You didn't go to a funeral last week.

ZOE: "Was...cremation. More environmental. Not take up so much ground with dead people."

TILLY: Okay, Zoe. We can play this later, over the weekend—

ZOE: "Burn and scatter ashes, dead body dirt mingle with dirt dirt."

TILLY: Tomorrow—you can tell me anything you want, and I'll believe it—

ZOE: "Tomorrow we get up crack-of-dawn, still dark. Your Mother come into room and wake us up, she say 'Get up girls, time to fly Disneyland.' Oh, we girls tired. We stay awake through whole night talking and laughing and having good time because we good good friends."

TILLY: Jeez.

ZOE: "You wear surprise from box..."

TILLY: *(Mildly interested)* What box?

ZOE: *(Senses TILLY's interest)* Box! ...Sent by *your father*."

TILLY: My dad?

ZOE: "Yes, sent box!"

TILLY: *(Intrigued)* ...What's in it?

ZOE: *(Tantalizes)* "Box shape so *odd*. Wrapping paper so *splendid*."

TILLY: From what store?

ZOE: *(Knows she's got her)* "Ho! Box make us crazy. We wonder and shake box all night, but Mother say not allowed to open until dawn. We die waiting for first sign of day. Oh, will day never come?"

TILLY: Tell me what's in it, already.

ZOE: "Must wait all night. In morning, your Mother call 'Wake up girls, time to get up and open box from dad.'"

TILLY: *(Playing along)* "Oh, it's just what I wanted."

ZOE: "Oh, so beautiful!"

TILLY: "Yeah...it's gorgeous."

ZOE: "Color good."

TILLY: "It's a gorgeous—" ...what?! Tell me what it is!

ZOE: ..."Bandeau!"

TILLY: What's that?

ZOE: "Bandeau. Very narrow shirt. Cover only across bosom. You hit of Disneyland in bandeau. Your Father one good shopper."

TILLY: No. My mother doesn't like my stomach rolls to show.

ZOE: "But bandeau gift from father so okay. We hurry into clothes and rush downstairs. Your Mother make pancakes and hash browns for farewell breakfast."

TILLY: Yeah, right. *(Mocks her mother's voice)* "Not for you, *Miss Big*. Not 'til you lose ten pounds."

(Brief pause. ZOE is shocked.)

ZOE: *(No accent.)* Who's "Miss Big"?

TILLY: Me.

ZOE: ...You really have to lose *ten pounds*?

TILLY: Really. I get an apple slice for dessert.

ZOE: What does Sam get?

TILLY: Pie. I don't get any dessert.

ZOE: I can bring you day-old from the bakery.

TILLY: A cake?

ZOE: Sure. Nobody buys day-old cake.

TILLY: With frosting?

ZOE: Okay.

TILLY: Two layers?

ZOE: Okay. And you can bring me your white umbrella.

TILLY: No, I can't.

ZOE: Why not?

TILLY: You know I'm not allowed to take it out of the house.

ZOE: If I'm bringing you a frosted cake—!

TILLY: Alright, already. *(Hears something)* Shh.

ZOE: What—?

TILLY: Oh, man—

JUDY: *(Off. Over)* You *said* you'd bring them.

ROSE: *(Off)* But I couldn't get any—my Dad quit. I got this instead—

(Enter JUDY and ROSE with a pizza.)

JUDY: I don't want it. ...Don't look now, creep invasion.

ROSE: What are you doing here?

ZOE: "Oh, look, Natasha. Rose come to take us Disneyland."

TILLY: *(To JUDY)* We're not here together, we're here separately.

ZOE: "We so silent in backseat of private airplane. Parents of Rose not even know we there. Yelena going to ride water slide. Tank you so much, Rose, you so generous."

ROSE: I'm not taking you anywhere, ever—you're nuts!

JUDY: Are you speaking English, Zoe?

ZOE: "Yelena speaking Russian."

ROSE: Completely insane.

ZOE: "Yelena not *in*sane. Yelena *out*sane."

ROSE: That's not even your name—

JUDY: A guy's looking for you, Zoe.

ZOE: *(To* TILLY, *disbelief)* Are *they* connected to the thing you have to do—?

TILLY: *(Pointedly)* You really have to go, Zoe. Your guy's here.

ROSE: How come every day you get picked up by a different terrorist?

ZOE: He's a taxi driver.

ROSE: He can be a taxi driver and still be a terrorist, you idiot.

ZOE: Terrorists are not taxi drivers, they're airplane pilots, you changeling.

ROSE: Don't call me names.

ZOE: Okay, *Rose.* Rose Rose Rose—

ROSE: Stop it.

ZOE: Be careful, Tilly. Changelings have been known to bite. *(Exits)*

JUDY: ...Aren't you going with her?

TILLY: No.

ROSE: Well, you can't stay here.

TILLY: We weren't together.

JUDY: You looked together.

TILLY: We were here accidentally at the same time. She tricks me. She's full of tricks. She's very advanced.

ROSE: Her clothes come from Savers.

TILLY: So what?

ROSE: I've seen her wearing my throw-away donations is what. And the taxpayers have to pay for her taxi rides to the college.

TILLY: Yeah, and you're really suffering, Rose, your family is starving to death.

(A little laugh escapes from JUDY.)

ROSE: I didn't say I was starving.

TILLY: *(Encouraged by JUDY's laugh)* Have you seen *me* wearing your throw-away donations?

ROSE: As if they'd fit you.

JUDY: What are you doing here, Tilly? This is our spot.

TILLY: Anybody can be here.

ROSE: Judy and I have important things to talk about.

TILLY: I won't listen.

ROSE: Fatty wants our pizza.

TILLY: That's pizza?

ROSE: In this *pizza* box? Yes, genius.

TILLY: Where did you get pizza?

ROSE: Delivery.

TILLY: To *school*?

ROSE: To anywhere. If you have money.

JUDY: Give it to her.

TILLY: *(Happy)* Really?

ROSE: *(Same time)* No.

JUDY: *(To* ROSE*)* Why not?

ROSE: It's for us.

JUDY: *(For the tenth time)* I don't want pizza, Rose. I want a cigarette.

ROSE: But my dad quit—

TILLY: Here, here! *(She reaches into her pocket and pulls out the cigarette. It's in tatters.)*

JUDY: What am I supposed to do with that?

TILLY: It got all smashed in my pocket.

ROSE: Because your pants are so tight.

TILLY: I thought it would be safe there.

JUDY: Get me another one.

TILLY: My Mom's purse is at work.

JUDY: Buy me some.

ROSE: She doesn't have any money.

JUDY: Then *you* buy me some.

ROSE: You have to be eighteen.

JUDY: The sleazy store will sell them to you.

ROSE: I'm not allowed in the sleazy store.

JUDY: Give me the money, and I'll go.

ROSE: You're going to go in the sleazy store?

JUDY: Sure, if you give me the money.

TILLY: If you give me the money, I'll go—

ROSE: I'm not going to give *you* money. *(Hands* JUDY *a dollar)* Here.

JUDY: It's *five* dollars.

ROSE: For cigarettes? Five?!

JUDY: That's what they cost.

(ROSE *hands* JUDY *more dollars.*)

ROSE: No wonder my Dad quit. *(Tentative)* ...When will you pay me back?

JUDY: *(Aghast)* Pay you back?

ROSE: *(Nervous)* ...Well, if you borrow money...you should pay it back.

JUDY: I never had to pay you back before.

ROSE: Well...maybe you should start—I mean the pizza was twelve dollars...

(Brief pause, then JUDY gets the pizza box, takes out a piece.)

ROSE: It's pepperoni, your favorite.

JUDY: *(She gives the pizza slice to* TILLY.) Here. Knock yourself out.

ROSE: What are you doing?

TILLY: Thanks. *(Eats hungrily)*

JUDY: She looked hungry.

ROSE: *(Attacking* TILLY, *as she doesn't dare criticize* JUDY) ...No wonder you weigh a ton.

JUDY: Slow down—you're going to choke to death.

ROSE: Yeah, and who'd carry the coffin—Superman is paralyzed. You got sauce on your face...You are so stupid.

TILLY: I'm not stupid.

ROSE: Oh no, you're a genius. "What's in the pizza box? A puppy?"

TILLY: I got a hundred on the quiz, that's how stupid I am. What did you get?

ROSE: If you got a hundred you cheated off your good friend Zoe.

JUDY: Are we going to go to the Fun Factory or not?

ROSE: *(Scuffling)* I—I need you to fix my outfit. You said you would.

JUDY: *(Pointedly)* I don't know when I can fix your outfit, Rose. I have to figure out a way to pay you back for the pizza I didn't even want.

ROSE: I didn't mean it—you don't have to pay me back—I didn't mean anything.

TILLY: *(To* JUDY*)* Want to go over to my house?

(ROSE *is threatened by* TILLY's *offer to* JUDY. *No pause)*

ROSE: And do what, play with *dolls?*

TILLY: I'm not even talking to you.

JUDY: *(Mildly curious)* What's at your house?

TILLY: We could do freak dancing.

ROSE: They don't call it that anymore. It's called freaking, freaking, you fat freak.

JUDY: You can't freak without boys.

TILLY: Yeah, my brother Sam. We could practice.

JUDY: You're going to freak with your *brother?*

TILLY: Why not?

(JUDY *snorts in disbelief.)*

ROSE: There are some things you don't do with a brother.

TILLY: What are they?

ROSE: You are stupid beyond belief.

TILLY: *(To* JUDY*)* Or we could...make up cool spy games and talk like Russians. It's really very fun. Me, you, and Sam.

ROSE: That sounds like something Zoe thought up. I think Tilly likes Zoe.

TILLY: I don't like her.

ROSE: You love her. Go practice freaking with Zoe.

TILLY: I...hate Zoe.

ROSE: Then why do you eat lunch with her?

TILLY: ...Because of her inheritance.

JUDY: *(Very into this)* What inheritance?

TILLY: *(Sensing* JUDY's *enthusiasm, expands the lie)* She's going to get a whole lot of money, and then she's going to spend it on her friends and give it away. To people who are her friends.

JUDY: Do you think she'd give me some?

TILLY: Well...when she gives me some, I can give you some.

JUDY: I'd rather get it directly—

ROSE: Wait a minute? Who died? I didn't hear about anybody who died. Somebody has to die for an inheritance.

TILLY: Her auntie. Her rich Russian auntie died. In Russia. She's going to get a lot. From her really rich dead auntie. Then she's going to give me a whole lot. She said.

ROSE: That's how we got money.

JUDY: How?

ROSE: ...Never mind.

JUDY: Come on, Rose! Tell.

ROSE: I'm not going to tell in front of her.... You want the rest of this? *(Pizza)*

TILLY: Okay.

ROSE: You can have it if you eat it someplace else.

*(*TILLY *considers this.)*

ROSE: Do you want it or not?

TILLY: Okay. Bye, Judy. Call me later. I'll tell you all about Zoe's money. *(She exits with pizza.)*

ROSE: *(Worried)* You're not going to call her, are you?

JUDY: I don't even know her number. Tell me how your family got rich.

ROSE: I—I need to talk to you about something else first.

JUDY: Talk to me about what? *(Brief pause) What*, Rose?!

ROSE: *(Scuffling)* You want to show me how to do my shirt first? The way you do it?

*(*JUDY *doesn't move or speak. Stands in defiance, waiting)*

ROSE: Okay, okay... You didn't say your mother was going to charge my mother.

JUDY: What are you talking about?

ROSE: For the makeover. The hundred dollars. She thought it was for free.

JUDY: For free? It was a two-hundred-dollar makeover.

ROSE: But it wasn't at the store, it was at our house.

JUDY: My mom had to leave work early—she had to take sick-time—

ROSE: But we thought it was for free.

JUDY: It took an hour and a half and your mother looked better than I've ever seen her—

ROSE: You haven't known her that long, she's looked good before—

JUDY: She got it for half price.

ROSE: She had to buy all the makeup.

JUDY: *Included*, she got the makeup included. Was she supposed to get the makeup for free, too?!

ROSE: My mother thought it was going to be free.

JUDY: Why did she think that?

ROSE: I don't know—just when you described it, it didn't sound like it was for money. All you said was that it was a beautiful dress and how my mother should let your mother do her hair and makeup. That's all you said.

JUDY: She looked great. She got a bargain.

ROSE: She looked nice. But you didn't say my mother was going to have to pay her a hundred dollars.

JUDY: Well, I sure didn't say it was for free. My mother can't work for free. Does *your father* work for free? Does your father...even work, or do people just die and leave him money?!

ROSE: My father didn't get the money, my mother did. Her aunt died.

JUDY: Yeah? That's the big secret? Rich people die?

ROSE: My Dad likes people to think he made the money at a job. That's why we moved here. Nobody knows us. Don't tell, okay?

JUDY: Who cares where money comes from as long as it comes? I wish I had a dead auntie.

ROSE: *(Takes a big breath, then)* My mother says you're using me.

JUDY: I'm not using you—

ROSE: No, I know you're not. Just my mother thinks so.

JUDY: —I introduced you to my friends. You couldn't have met those guys without me.

ROSE: Yeah, but—

JUDY: They're seventh grade. It's hard to meet those guys. Didn't you like meeting them?

ROSE: I paid for the games.

JUDY: You played them.

ROSE: I paid for yours, too.

JUDY: So I could play with you. You won most of them.

ROSE: We could do Dutch treat next time.

JUDY: What is that? Is that some gay thing?

ROSE: No. It means everybody pays for herself.

JUDY: *(Brief pause, calculating, very sincere)* ...Okay... okay, we'll do it the Dutch way. But then, you know, Rose, there's a lot of places I can't go. I can't go to the Fun Factory if it's everybody has to pay for herself, so you're going to have to go by yourself. And I'll just have to go home.

ROSE: I can't go by myself.

JUDY: Well, I can't go. Because I don't have any money. You can just go home. *(She starts to exit.)*

ROSE: Hey, where are you going? Don't be mad—

JUDY: I'm not mad. I just don't have any money for the Fun Factory.

ROSE: Wait. We can go...for a little while.

JUDY: And you'll pay?

ROSE: For a little while. And then we can go over to my house.

JUDY: I don't want to see your mother if she thinks I'm using you. It's too hurtful.

ROSE: ...She doesn't. She likes you. She really likes you.

Scene 2

(Next day, TILLY *and* ZOE. *Behind bleachers. A cake box; a large, closed, white umbrella.* TILLY *hurries to finish the cake.* ZOE *is very agitated.)*

ZOE: Why? Why can't it happen here? It can *so* happen here. We have power plants just like they have power plants.

TILLY: It can't happen here, because it never happens here, and it isn't going to happen here. It always happens there. It never happens here.

*(*ZOE *walks under the bleachers, frightened.)*

ZOE: All the electricity for millions and millions and millions of people—

TILLY: *(Desperate to end* ZOE's *episode of panic)* It wasn't terrorist planes, Zoe, it was lightning, okay? It was just lightning.

ZOE: Little children stuck in dark elevators with no hope of escape—

TILLY: Everybody is fine now, you don't have to still be worrying.

ZOE: Swallowed up by the darkness in a darkened elevator.

TILLY: They used their matches!

ZOE: ...They did?

TILLY: *(Talking* ZOE *down)* ...You got your matches?

ZOE: Yes.

TILLY: You're fine, Zoe, you got your matches, you're fine.

ZOE: ...They had their matches. They weren't in the dark.

TILLY: They were fine.

(ZOE *glances to see if anybody is coming.*)

ZOE: Where are they? I have to go soon.

TILLY: I don't know. They should be here—they always come here.

ZOE: *(She looks in cake box)* What happened to the rest of the cake?

TILLY: What rest?

ZOE: *(Amazed)* You ate it all? *(She looks under a piece of tissue in the box.)*

TILLY: What are you doing?!

ZOE: Nothing—I was just seeing if it was really all gone.

TILLY: ...I thought you were going to take some.

ZOE: There isn't any to take.

TILLY: Well, you didn't say you wanted some. *(She tosses box in garbage can.)*

ZOE: I didn't want some—I was just seeing. *(She studies TILLY's stomach.)* Where did it go?

TILLY: Where do you think it went?!

ZOE: Can I feel your stomach?

TILLY: Don't push on it.

ZOE: I won't push. Wow. Not even puffy.

TILLY: Don't make fun of me.

ZOE: I'm not. I'm very impressed. You must be stuffed to pain.

TILLY: I'm not stuffed at all. I never get stuffed.

ZOE: You break all the rules of volume and capacity. Will you be my project? I need a math project at college.

TILLY: No, those college kids will laugh at me.

ZOE: Nobody laughs at math—I can measure your stomach, then I can measure the food, and we can have twice as much food as ought to fit into your stomach, and then—

TILLY: Stop it stop it stop it!

ZOE: I'm trying to find out how much you can eat. It's just math.

TILLY: I can eat a whole lot, okay?

ZOE: Could you eat a whole other cake?

TILLY: You *have* a whole other cake?

ZOE: No, but I can bring two tomorrow.

TILLY: Will your Dad let you?

ZOE: If I tell him it's for math.

TILLY: I never get enough cake. They give me the smallest piece because I'm the fattest kid. And it's only enough to get my cake needs going. They starve me. Everybody hates me because I'm fat.

ZOE: I don't.

TILLY: You don't count. Sam makes fun of me and Mom puts a lock on the freezer.

ZOE: *(Aghast)* I don't count?

TILLY: Dad doesn't hate me, but he's the only one. Mom says because he doesn't love me, that's why he doesn't hate me—

ZOE: Why don't I count? I count.

TILLY: You don't count because if I was a fat ax-murderer you'd still be friends with me.

ZOE: That means I should count more.

TILLY: Okay, Zoe. You can count. You can count more.

ZOE: You could come live with me.

TILLY: I'm going to go live with my Dad. As soon as he gets a bigger place. *He* doesn't call me names.

ZOE: Your mother doesn't call you names.

TILLY: She doesn't when people are around.

ZOE: What does she call you?

TILLY: The newest one is really bad. I don't want to say it.

ZOE: "Miss Big?"

TILLY: Worse.

ZOE: *(Whispers)* Is it "Fatty?"

TILLY: That was the worst one for a while.

ZOE: I can't think of anything worse than Fatty.

TILLY: ...Promise you won't tell.

ZOE: Who would I tell? Nobody talks to me.

TILLY: Promise!

ZOE: I promise I won't tell.

TILLY: She calls me Garbage Belly.

ZOE: ...Garbage Belly?

TILLY: Yeah, pretty terrible, huh?

ZOE: *(Thrilled by the name)* That's like an environmental machine, helping the planet get rid of its detritus— like a tilapia swimming along the bottom of the ocean cleaning it up for the other fish. "Thank you, Tilly, for cleaning up the environment. *(A cheer)* "Garbage Belly, Garbage Belly. Hooray for Garbage Belly."

TILLY: Jeez, stop it.

ZOE: "Tilly, the human trash compactor!"

TILLY: Stop it right now—

ZOE: I like to say it.

TILLY: Don't say it—and don't tell anybody.

ZOE: Okay, but I think it's very cool.

TILLY: It is not cool to be the fattest kid in America.

ZOE: There's a guy at my college fatter than you.

TILLY: Really?

ZOE: Yes, but I don't think he can eat two cakes. I watched him. He ate just normal.

TILLY: Everybody eats normal when they're being watched.

ZOE: *(Touching* TILLY's *stomach)* Amazing. Just like a trash compactor.

TILLY: Stop it, and don't let it slip out when they get here.

ZOE: Why do I have to talk to them?

TILLY: Just be nice to Judy. Play Russians with her, okay?

ZOE: Did you steal another cigarette for her?

TILLY: None of your business.

ZOE: She gave me this. *(She takes out a greeting card.)* "Rain or shine, you are my sweetest Valentine." Love Judy.

TILLY: Why did she give you a Valentine?

ZOE: You tell me.

TILLY: It isn't Valentine's Day.

ZOE: Why would she give me a Valentine even if it *was* Valentine's Day? She's never even talked to me. She slipped it on my desk when she went to the girls' room.

TILLY: *(Realizes)* She's trying to make friends with you!

ZOE: *(Thinks* TILLY *is jealous of the card)* Do you want it? You can have it.

TILLY: I don't want it.

ZOE: Hey, it's no big thing. It's probably just a leftover one from last year.

TILLY: Zoe, I don't care about the card.

ZOE: *(Worried)* ...Do you like her more than you like me?

TILLY: I don't like her.

ZOE: *(Amazed and happy)* You don't?

TILLY: No, I don't like her, okay?

ZOE: Hooray, hooray, I thought you liked her—

TILLY: I don't. I don't care who she gives cards to.

ZOE: Then why are you trying to be friends with her?

*(*TILLY *doesn't reply.)*

ZOE: Is it because you think she's pretty?

TILLY: Do you think she's pretty?

ZOE: A little, I do.

TILLY: So does my mother. Jeez, I don't see it. "Look at Judy, she's so pretty, why can't you be like Judy?"

ZOE: Does your mother want you to freak boys with your butt, too?

TILLY: *(Shudders.)* She's disgusting. She looks like viruses and pus to me.

*(*ZOE *mock dances, sings, shakes her behind exaggeratedly.)*

ZOE: "Uh uh uh uh uh uh uh uh uh. Uh uh uh uh uh uh uh uh uh. UH! Freak my butt!" How was that?

TILLY: Just like Judy.

ZOE: You try it.

TILLY: No—it's disgusting.

ZOE: You have to do it someday.

TILLY: No, I don't. Neither do you.

ZOE: Yes. Someday when I'm older I want to do it. Just not yet.

TILLY: I never want to do it. I'll always stay like this and then nobody will make me.

ZOE: Stay like what?

TILLY: Stay fat.

ZOE: You're pretty.

TILLY: I'm pretty fat.

ZOE: I like how you look.

TILLY: You like how pigs look, too?

ZOE: Pigs are very smart.

TILLY: Jeez—

ZOE: No, I didn't mean you look like a pig. I just meant. ...I don't know what I meant. There's different kinds of pretty, that's all I meant.

TILLY: Yeah and nobody likes my kind and I don't care.

ZOE: Is it because of boys? Because boys like her? Is that why you want to be friends with her?

TILLY: I'm not going to be friends with her—I don't like her—I don't think she's pretty—okay? Jeez—

ZOE: Okay. ...But then what's going on—?

TILLY: *(To distract, she gets the umbrella.)* Here, I brought this. You said you wanted it. You can take it with you. Just bring it back tomorrow. And don't let my mother know.

ZOE: You're not going to tell me?

TILLY: ...I'll tell you when it's over... What are you going to do with the umbrella?

(ZOE *does an umbrella twirl and dance.*)

ZOE: *(Russian game)* "...Ho, Natasha—magic shield protect us from terrorists. Must disguise magic shield so no one will try to steal." *(Draws on it with gold glitter glue)* "Yelena and Natasha safe from all attacks."

TILLY: Hey, what are you doing—? Don't do that.

ZOE: "Must disguise shield."

TILLY: That's glue!

ZOE: "We turn magic shield into thing of beauty for Natasha."

TILLY: What am I going to tell my mother?

ZOE: *(No accent.)* Tilly—Two cakes. I'm bringing you two cakes.

TILLY: Alright, alight. ...I'll tell my mother I lost it.... Yeah, she'll believe that. "You'd lose your head if it wasn't tied on."

ZOE: It's not tied on, it's connected with connective tissue.

TILLY: She gives me white things then yells at me when I get them dirty.

ZOE: White...and gold.

TILLY: Then she calls me a slob. "You fat slob."

ZOE: Oh... That's much worse than Garbage Belly.

TILLY: Stop saying it.

ZOE: You're not a slob, Tilly. And there's worse things than being fat.

TILLY: Thanks.

ZOE: You should tell her. Tell your mother there's worse things.

TILLY: *(Very determined.)* I'm not going to tell her. I'm going to show her.

(ZOE shows the gold stars.)

TILLY: Nice.

ZOE: "Take shield. Hold in front of you. No one ever make fun of Natasha again. Natasha so slim now, behind shield."

TILLY: That's because you can't see me. *(She peeks out from behind the umbrella.)*

(ZOE gasps.)

TILLY: What?

ZOE: Oh. *(Takes umbrella, subdued)* My mother used to do that. Peek around the umbrella. She would open a huge umbrella and let me crawl under it.

TILLY: You can't remember your mother.

ZOE: A huge white cloud umbrella with gold stars... then...a giant lady face peeks around the cloud— *(Sings)* Rock-a-bye Zoe in the tree top, when the wind blows the cradle will rock...

TILLY: It must have been a dream.

ZOE: It feels like a memory.

(Enter ROSE and JUDY.)

JUDY: Hey, Zoe. We were waiting for you by your taxi stand.

ROSE: *I* wasn't waiting. Your terrorist is here.

ZOE: He's early.

ROSE: *(Re umbrella)* Is that for some hurricane?

ZOE: "This secret." *(She closes and puts aside the umbrella.)*

JUDY: I got something for you.

ZOE: Another Valentine's Day card?

ROSE: What?

(ZOE *holds up the card.*)

ROSE: *(Disbelief)* Why did you give her a card?

JUDY: I was just being nice. Here.

(JUDY *gives* ZOE *a notebook.*)

ZOE: "Ho, Yelena love presents."

ROSE: *(To* JUDY*)* Don't give her that.

JUDY: She needs it; all her papers are loose.

ROSE: I thought it was for you.

JUDY: I already have one.

ROSE: Oh, man—

ZOE: "Yelena love new notebook."

JUDY: It's the good kind. It costs seven dollars at Longs.

ROSE: Where she *didn't* get it.

ZOE: "Where Judy get nice notebook?"

ROSE: She found it in the garbage can in my room.

ZOE: "Why Rose put nice notebook in garbage can?"

ROSE: Because I drew on it with magic marker so I got a new one.

JUDY: Here's a punch, too. So you can put your loose papers in it.

ROSE: No. I want the punch back.

JUDY: Oh come on—you won't use it. You got that new electric one that does three holes at once.

ZOE: "Oh, tank you, Rose. Yelena tank you so much for fabulous hole punch and notebook. Never before has Yelena had such a nice hole punch."

ROSE: Don't thank me. Thank my garbage can.

JUDY: *(Gently)* Come on, Rose. We're only going to be here for a little while, and then we'll go. Okaay? *(To others)* ...Rose always has very interesting things in her garbage can.

TILLY: Really?

ROSE: Don't get excited, Fatty. Not food.

ZOE: "We not use name 'Fatty'!"

TILLY: *(To* ZOE*)* You promised—!

ROSE: Lard Behind?

TILLY: *(Panicking)* What are you doing—?!

ZOE: *(Over)* "Natasha."

TILLY: Oh. *(Relieved.)* ...Yeah, I'm Natasha...in the fun game we play. Zoe's Yelena.

ZOE: "Yelena fix notebook good like new." *(She glitters it.)*

ROSE: Mister Tanaka will kill you if you get glitter in the room.

ZOE: "He so happy with beautiful notebook he pass out glitter to all students."

JUDY: Yeah, that looks great.

ROSE: It looks like about second grade.

JUDY: It's pretty.

ROSE: Come on. You don't like this baby stuff.

TILLY: Hey—I brought you a cigarette.

JUDY: Great. *(Takes it)*

ZOE: "Smoking not allowed."

ROSE: You can't make the rules for here.

JUDY: I hate smoking.

TILLY & ROSE: What?

JUDY: It's a filthy habit.

ZOE: "Mean capitalists get rich because people have smoking weaknesses."

JUDY: Yeah, it's gross. But I have to smoke to stay thin.

ROSE: Otherwise you'd be as fat as Tubbo.

ZOE: *(Correcting)* "Natasha!"

JUDY: Whenever I want cake or chocolate, I have to smoke.

ROSE: *(To TILLY)* Maybe you should try that.

JUDY: I'm quitting even though I'm addicted. *(She rips up cigarette.)*

TILLY: I had to sneak that out of my mother's purse while she was in the shower. It was creepy, and you just tore it up.

JUDY: You shouldn't rip off your own mother.

TILLY: But—

ROSE: *(Over)* You didn't mind *me* ripping off my own father.

JUDY: *(To ROSE)* And now...you don't have to, ever again. *(To ZOE)* What's the secret about the umbrella?

ZOE: "Magic shield protect Russians from terrorists. Must keep out of hands of ruthless American scientists."

(JUDY takes the umbrella and starts to play her version of ZOE's game.)

JUDY: "I got it, Men. I got the Russians' shield."

ZOE: "Oh, no, Natasha. American spies steal Russian shield. Now we not protected!"

ROSE: *(Disbelief)* What are you doing?

JUDY: *(To ROSE)* "We can use the shield to protect America."

ROSE: I don't want to play this.

JUDY: Come on, it might be fun.

ROSE: Forget it.

JUDY: Suit yourself. *(Playing)* "I'm hiding the shield far from the Russian scientists so that they can never steal it back."

ZOE: "Come, *Natasha*. We must force way into American compound. You go in front, I break back window, climb inside. Surprise them."

TILLY: "Which way is front?"

ZOE: "Shhh, I see them. Halt! I have weapon."

JUDY: "Your weapon is powerless against the magic shield, Yelena."

ZOE: *(To* TILLY*)* "Ho. She right."

(JUDY *hides under the bleachers.)*

ZOE: "We must get shield, Natasha. All Russian future depend on it."

ROSE: Well, I guess we know why we beat the Russians. They lost their big umbrella.

ZOE: *(To* TILLY*)* "Perhaps we can bribe greedy American with offer of big bucks for umbrella."

ROSE: You mean you'd pay money for it?

ZOE: "Shield priceless. Will pay any amount."

JUDY: I thought you weren't playing.

ROSE: ...How much will you pay if I can get the umbrella back?

ZOE: "We pay big big bucks."

ROSE: *(Entering game)* Okay. "I'll get you back the magic umbrella. As soon as you get me a hundred dollars."

JUDY: Jeez, Rose—

ROSE: "I'll tell my supervisor the magic umbrella was... stolen in a laboratory fire. One hundred dollars and the umbrella is yours."

ZOE: "Natasha! Give me one hundred American dollars to buy off American spy."

TILLY: "Here."

(TILLY *hands rock to* ZOE.)

ZOE: "Tank you. Here."

ROSE: What's this?

ZOE: "This one hundred American dollars."

ROSE: It's a rock.

JUDY: It's pretend, Rose.

ROSE: I don't want pretend. I need a real hundred dollars, and then I'll get you the umbrella.

TILLY: Where are we supposed to get a real hundred dollars?

ROSE: From an *heiress*. Don't you know an *heiress* with a dead rich aunt?

ZOE: *(Shocked)* Tilly—?

ROSE: If somebody is an heiress she can get a hundred dollars right away—

TILLY: *(To cover)* Jeez— That's ridiculous— How are kids, even rich kids supposed to get a hundred dollars—I never heard anything so silly—Zoe, it's past time for you to go.

ZOE: Why did you tell them?

TILLY: It's okay, don't worry about it. *(Pointedly)* They'll keep your secret. About how you're going to get a big inheritance. Really soon.

JUDY: Yeah, we can keep a secret.

TILLY: Your taxi guy's here. You don't want to make him wait.

ROSE: He can drive you to the bank to get the money—

ZOE: I have to go. I'll talk to you, later, Tilly. *(She exits.)*

JUDY: Rose, why did you do that?

ROSE: Why did I do what?

JUDY: You said heiress—you told her to go to the bank—

ROSE: My mother wants her money back.

JUDY: Now she thinks we were playing with her for her inheritance money.

ROSE: We were.

JUDY: You didn't even try—you sat there and pouted.

ROSE: *(Upset)* You were taking forever. I couldn't stand it. How can you stand to be around them? *(Re TILLY)* Look at her—

JUDY: You can't just ask somebody for a hundred dollars without being nice to them first.

ROSE: You're changing all the rules—you can't change the rules.

JUDY: What rules?

ROSE: You didn't say you were going to give her the stuff from my room.

JUDY: How else is she going to like us? I had to give her that stuff. What's the big deal? You were throwing it away—

ROSE: The big deal is I thought I was giving it to you.

JUDY: It doesn't make any difference.

ROSE: *(Hurt)* You stopped smoking for her.

JUDY: I just said that—I didn't really stop.

ROSE: *(Amazed)* You didn't?

JUDY: No, I didn't.

ROSE: ...Oh.

JUDY: I'm just trying to get the money.

ROSE: Oh... Okay.

TILLY: *(She does not understand what they're talking about, but tries to use what's she heard to drive a wedge between them.)* You—you blew it, Rose. Zoe doesn't want anybody to know about her money.

ROSE: Why not? Everybody knows about my money.

TILLY: You tell everybody you go to Disneyland every weekend—you tell everybody you have a big car and a big house and lots of money. Zoe wants to be able to do really nice things for other people. Secretly.

ROSE: I do nice things. I gave her all that nice stuff.

TILLY: You tried to take it back. You are a tightwad. Holding tight to your money wad.

ROSE: You would, too, if you had any. You don't know that because you don't have any. If you had any, you'd know.

TILLY: *(To JUDY)* Zoe's not like that.

ROSE: She's a freak.

TILLY: She's not a freak. She's just a really nice person. She's going to be rich, Judy. If somebody needed some money, a hundred dollars or something, somebody who was her friend, she'd give it to her. It's going to be really fun to be friends with a *generous* rich girl. We could go to my house and call her up—

ROSE: Nobody's going over to your house, so just forget it. Come on.

(JUDY uses the situation to her advantage.)

JUDY: ...Where are we going to go, Rose?

ROSE: My house. We can listen to music.

JUDY: We did that yesterday.

ROSE: ...We'll go to the Fun Factory. I'll pay for the games.

JUDY: You will?

ROSE: ...Yes?

JUDY: Great. Bye, Tilly.

(JUDY and ROSE exit. TILLY remains, having failed again to get JUDY to her house.)

Scene 3

(Next day. Bleachers. Umbrella. TILLY, nervously waits. Enter JUDY.)

JUDY: Where is she?

TILLY: She's coming. I told her to.

JUDY: (Picks up umbrella) ...You guys have really ruined this umbrella. It probably leaks now.

TILLY: Where's Rose?

JUDY: Rose is waiting for me at a designated spot. (Brief pause) She's so stupid... (Rhetorical) Do you have any idea how fast a hundred dollars is gone?

TILLY: ...No.

JUDY: Neither does Rose.

TILLY: ...I really like your outfit.

JUDY: It won't fit you.

TILLY: No, I know. I don't want it or anything. I just like it. To admire it.

JUDY: (Realizes) Oh—are you gay or something?

TILLY: I'm not gay.

JUDY: Are you sure?

TILLY: I don't think so.

JUDY: I don't think I am either. My mom says sometimes you don't know until you're older.

TILLY: Is she gay?

JUDY: Her sister. That's how come I'm not a homophobe. We love my auntie.

TILLY: I have a gay uncle. Maybe we should introduce them.

JUDY: Why would we do that?

TILLY: I don't know. Here. (*She gives her a $20 bill.*) This is for you.

JUDY: Why?

TILLY: You like money.

JUDY: Why do you have twenty dollars?

TILLY: I brought it for you.

JUDY: Thanks. Will you bring it for me again tomorrow?

TILLY: ...I don't know, I could try maybe. And then maybe you could get that hundred dollars you need.

JUDY: I don't need it. Rose needs it.

TILLY: You could start to save it up.

JUDY: Save it up? How do you do that? One movie, one bag of popcorn, one soda, gone! Like it was never there. It's only enough to spend, nothing left to save.

TILLY: ...I have a brother.

JUDY: Does he have money?

TILLY: No. But you'd like him. He's older.

JUDY: Is he anything like you?

TILLY: What do you mean? Do you mean is he fat? He's not fat. He's cute. Do you want to come over to meet him?

JUDY: I don't want any more boyfriends. When is Zoe coming?

TILLY: Soon, she'll be here soon. You could do freaking with my brother.

JUDY: Stop with your brother, already. I get plenty of boys—

TILLY: But he's fourteen, he's ninth grade—

JUDY: I don't need you fixing me up.

TILLY: No, I know.

JUDY: I'm sick of boys...I may not even go to the dance.

TILLY: If you needed a ride, my mother could drive us.

JUDY: Don't call us, we'll call you.

TILLY: You could come over to my house, and we could leave from there.

JUDY: Jeez.

(JUDY *sidles away with the umbrella. Brief pause as* TILLY *tries to figure out a new approach.*)

TILLY: ...I liked your story he read.

JUDY: *(Lying)* That wasn't my story.

TILLY: Where did you get the idea for it? Are *you* going to be evicted?

JUDY: I said it isn't mine--we're not getting evicted. It was somebody else's story.

TILLY: But the girl's mother did makeovers.

JUDY: So what?! Somebody else can put that in a story. It wasn't my story.

TILLY: Oh. Well. I didn't really like it that much anyway.

JUDY: ...Why not?

TILLY: I couldn't tell how anything happened. Where did the money come from for the bus ticket?

JUDY: Out of the safe.

TILLY: No—where did it come from *before* the safe—how did it get *into* the safe?

JUDY: ...I don't know...I didn't hear that part.

TILLY: I don't think it was there. I listened very hard. It wasn't very complete.

JUDY: Well it must have been *mostly complete* or Mister Tanaka wouldn't have read it. So he must have thought it was pretty complete.

TILLY: Yeah... What are you going to do with the umbrella?

JUDY: Whatever Zoe wants.

TILLY: It's my umbrella, you know.

JUDY: Then take it! Jeez.

TILLY: Oh, no, I didn't mean you had to give it to me.

JUDY: Then why did you bring it up whose umbrella it is?

TILLY: I don't know. Do you want to—

JUDY: No!

TILLY: We could play Russians. "Hello, Yelena. Hello, Natasha? That nice umbrella."

JUDY: (*A disbelieving expulsion of air*) Forget it.

(ZOE *enters, takes the umbrella.*)

ZOE: "Magic shield transport us to Planet Outer Space. Fast, fast, G-force, G-force. Face get so flat!" *(Makes sounds of jet propulsion)*

JUDY: "Oh, the G-force is flattening my face."

ZOE: "G-force strong. Face so flat. Eeeeeeee."

ZOE & JUDY: *(Flat-faces)* Eeeeeeeeeeeeee.

ZOE: "Pain of G-force too big. Isn't it big, Tilly?"

TILLY: *(To* JUDY*)* Why are you being a Russian? Aren't you supposed to be the American?

JUDY: Well, I guess I'm a Russian today, okay?!

TILLY: No, I didn't mean anything—

ZOE: *(For* TILLY*)* "We all three so *weightless*. Like feathers. Nobody overweight in outer space. Floating and floating. Try floating, Natasha. We floating in the beautiful planet outer space."

JUDY: "Yes! Look at those cool outer space *bleachers*."

ZOE: "Ho. Not bleachers. Strange seating arrangement extra terrestrials have for viewing at ritual site."

JUDY: Hey, I have an idea— Let's go to the mall and get some planet outer space outfits.

ZOE: They have those?

JUDY: They have everything. We'll get new outfits.

ZOE: I don't have any money.

JUDY: Yet. You don't have any money "yet".

ZOE: ...I don't have any money.

JUDY: Let's go anyway. I have twenty dollars.

TILLY: Hey—

JUDY: What? I *don't* have twenty dollars? Somebody wants their twenty dollars back?!

TILLY: No—I just—Can I go?

JUDY: Well, it's only twenty dollars. How far does twenty dollars go? Just enough to get some makeup for Zoe. I can make you over.

ZOE: "Ho. Yelena get one makeover! How you going fix up Yelena?"

JUDY: *(Gazes at her)* Wow. Where do I start? Put that down.

(JUDY takes away the umbrella and begins to remake ZOE: the things she does to ZOE, TILLY does to herself.)

JUDY: Take off your belt, here, untuck your shirt, let me do it. Put this on the outside. Roll up your pants. *(She rolls down ZOE's socks.)* Push your hair out of your face. You need to get some hair spray. Push your sleeves up. That's better.

ZOE: "Yelena one model."

(ZOE does an awkward model walk. TILLY and JUDY study her.)

TILLY: She looks cool. How come? It's all the same stuff.

JUDY: It looks like she gave it some thought. That's what style is. You give it some thought. You don't just grab yesterday's dirty clothes from the pile.

TILLY: *(Guilty)* I didn't do that!

JUDY: Style isn't about money. Some of the richest people have zero style.

TILLY: Do you want to come to my house and make me over?

JUDY: *(To ZOE, after a dismissive glance at TILLY)* Now all those college boys will talk to you.

ZOE: I don't want them to talk to me.

JUDY: You could freak with them.

ZOE: I don't know how.

JUDY: You want to learn?

(JUDY *demonstrates a sexy dance.* TILLY *turns away in disgust.* ZOE *is alert, trying to understand* TILLY.)

TILLY: (*Forcing herself*) Hey, I have an idea. I have a great idea.

ZOE: What's your great idea, Tilly?

TILLY: Judy can teach you how to dance at my house. You can come over before dinner and teach her. My brother's there. He can help.

JUDY: I don't think so.

(TILLY *gives a desperate look to* ZOE.)

ZOE: ...Yes we should. It makes more sense to learn how to dance inside a house. Where there's some music to listen to.

JUDY: Okay. Let's go.

ZOE: Go get Rose.

TILLY: No—

ZOE: So we all have a partner. You two can meet us. It's the yellow house in the middle of the block behind the school. Go invite Rose.

JUDY: I'll invite her. But maybe we'll be lucky and she won't be able to come. (*Exits*)

TILLY: Why did you do that? Rose will get in my way.

ZOE: I need to find out what you're up to. What are you up to?

TILLY: I—I can't tell you. But don't come over, okay? Promise me you won't come over.

ZOE: Don't do it, Tilly, whatever it is. I got cakes. Come over to my house and you can eat them—

TILLY: (*Tempted, but...*) No. I have to do this. (*Exiting*)

ZOE: Where are you going?

TILLY: I got to get everything ready.

(ZOE, *alone for a minute, opens the umbrella, puts it on the ground, sits under it.*)

ZOE: "Rock a bye baby, in the tree top—" *(Hears something)*

ROSE: *(Off)* Where were you? I waited and waited.

(ZOE *exits.*)

JUDY: *(Off)* I was coming—I was just coming to get you.

ROSE: Where are they? They were here, I know they were.

JUDY: Nobody's here but us.

ROSE: I waited and waited. Why didn't you come?

JUDY: I was coming right now. What's the matter with you?

ROSE: It was creepy. All the buses are gone even.

JUDY: Why didn't you just go home? No big deal.

ROSE: I couldn't go home...I got these. *(She hands* JUDY *a pack of cigarettes.)* They're for you.

JUDY: Thanks.

ROSE: I couldn't take them home.

JUDY: I don't see why not.

ROSE: Because I swiped them. It was creepy, it's not like swiping a bag of chips, the guy watches them really close. I've had them in my pocket since lunch.

JUDY: Why didn't you just give them to me?

ROSE: I didn't want anybody to see. Where were you all this time?

JUDY: Oh, well, first I was just talking to Mister Tanaka about my story...that took a while...then I forgot. I forgot I told you to wait by the buses, and I came here and waited for you. Then I remembered and was coming to look for you. By the buses.

ROSE: *(Doesn't quite believe it)* ...What did Mister Tanaka say?

JUDY: He said...I should figure out how the money got in the safe.

ROSE: Oh. I never thought of that.

JUDY: I didn't either or I would have put it in the story.

ROSE: Do you like the cigarettes?

JUDY: Yeah, they're great. You want one?

ROSE: No. *(Brief pause)* You want to go to play games?

JUDY: No.

ROSE: Where do you want to go?

JUDY: Home.

ROSE: Okay, let's go.

JUDY: You can't come...I have to talk to my Mom about some stuff.

ROSE: Your mother doesn't get home until eight.

JUDY: I need to rewrite my story.

ROSE: You're not going some place without me, are you?

JUDY: I'm not going any place.

ROSE: You swear?

JUDY: Sure. I'll call you later. After dinner. Okay?

ROSE: ...I better call you.

JUDY: Why? Can't I call your house any more?

ROSE: No, you can. It's just...my mother likes me to not get calls...so I have to sneak them now.

JUDY: Your mother hates me, doesn't she?

ROSE: No, she doesn't. She didn't say that.

JUDY: Your mother doesn't want me to call up. That's it, isn't it?

ROSE: No, it's the reason I said. Here. *(From her pocket, a ring)* This is for you. It's a present.

JUDY: *(Amazed by the ring)* How come you didn't wrap it up?

ROSE: Because...it's a present I already had. I didn't buy it new. So I didn't get a box.

JUDY: What are the stones?

ROSE: They're opals. They're very valuable. And it's gold.

JUDY: *(Putting on the ring, it's too big)* Did it fit *you*?

ROSE: Oh... No. It was my mother's. I never got it made smaller for me is why it's still so big.

JUDY: *(Pause, suspicious)* Is it *still* your mother's?

ROSE: *(Guilty)* What do you mean?

JUDY: Did you steal it?

ROSE: *(Lying)* ...No.

JUDY: *(She puts the ring on a fatter finger)* Thanks, Rose. Thanks a lot.

ROSE: *(Worried)* Are you going to wear it?

JUDY: You bet I'm going to wear it. It's gorgeous.

ROSE: But it doesn't fit the right finger.

JUDY: I'll get it made smaller.

ROSE: But maybe you should just sell it. It's worth a lot.

JUDY: How much?

ROSE: ...Maybe thousands. You could sell it and buy a ring that fits.

JUDY: I like this one.

ROSE: No, you should sell this one. And then you could use some of the money to pay back my mother.

JUDY: *(Finally understands)* Oh, man—

ROSE: No—and then you could keep the rest of the money after you sell it.

JUDY: Where would I sell it—? I don't know how to sell jewelry—

ROSE: You could get your mother to do it. At a place. They stay open late—you could go tonight—

JUDY: A pawn shop?! My mother doesn't go to pawn shops. We don't do that—we don't know how to do that.

ROSE: You don't?

JUDY: No, we don't. What do you think we are?!

ROSE: No, I just meant—My mother wants her money back.

JUDY: Is that why you gave me this—?

ROSE: I have to get her money back. They're going to send me to a different school. With my own kind. I'm going to have to be with my own kind. I don't want to.

JUDY: Take it.

ROSE: If I get her the money back, she'll see you and your mother *aren't* a couple of lowlifes, and maybe I can stay. I have to get the money back or they're going to send me away.

JUDY: Here.

(JUDY returns the ring to ROSE.)

ROSE: But—

JUDY: Take it. I don't want your mother's ring. I'll get her money.

Scene 4

(TILLY *is watching. Lights up on a silhouette.* JUDY *freak dances. Lights down on silhouette.* TILLY *watches.*)

(*Blackout*)

END OF ACT ONE

ACT TWO

Scene 5

(The next day. The bleachers. TILLY *comes on crying, furious.* ZOE *follows.)*

ZOE: It wasn't that bad.

TILLY: Shut up.

ZOE: You don't have to be embarrassed.

TILLY: What do you know about it?

ZOE: Nobody will remember. I forgot already.

TILLY: Yeah, the number is too enormous to remember.

ZOE: Nobody cares how much you weigh.

TILLY: He should have told us, he should have told us it was today. Then I could have stayed home and pretended I was sick.

ZOE: He didn't tell us because it's no big thing. They do it every fall. It's no big thing.

TILLY: It's no big thing unless you're huge, then it's a big thing. You don't know Zoe, you don't know anything. They don't make fun of you, they don't call you names—

ZOE: They make fun of me and call me names all the time. Except at college where nobody talks to me at all. Please stop crying. It doesn't make sense to be so crying about this. They weighed you *last year*, you didn't cry like this. You aren't that much fatter.

TILLY: Leave me alone.

ZOE: I'm not mad at you, you know. I should be really mad at you.

TILLY: For what?

ZOE: For telling Judy and Rose I was going to get rich.

TILLY: Why should you be mad for that? It's your stupid game.

ZOE: Yeah, you and me know it's a game, but now you got them believing I'm going to get rich.... It's pretty funny, though, how nice Judy is to me. I guess she's waiting for me to give her a big pile of money. Ha!

TILLY: Who cares who Judy is nice to. I don't care. I hate her.

ZOE: *(Brief pause)* Did something happen at your house last night? Is that why you're so crying?

TILLY: Shit. Shit shit shit.

ZOE: Did Judy come over?

TILLY: Yeah, she came over. We had a really good time— My mother loves her! My mother loves her a whole lot more than she loves me, she's not a big fat slob, she's perfect—

ZOE: I'm sorry, Tilly.

TILLY: I wanted Mom to see, she had to see...I put on a C D and Judy and Sam started to freak, rubbing her skinny butt against Sam's pants, touching herself, rubbing her hands across her front, rubbing her butt against Sam, right in front of me and Mom. And then Sam squirted—I could tell from his face, and there was a stain on his pants. See, Mom, see? Isn't she disgusting? I looked over...and Mom was laughing.

She was laughing. She thought it was cute. She thought it was cute.

ZOE: Oh no...

TILLY: *(Over)* "Why can't you look like that, Tilly. Why can't you dress like that, Tilly? Why can't you dance like *that*, Tilly?"

ZOE: Sam freaked her butt?

TILLY: Then they just pretended it didn't happen.

ZOE: Is that why you were being nice to her? So she'd come over to your house? So your mother could see her freak dance with Sam?

TILLY: I wanted to make her see.

ZOE: ...My father says the girl could be anything. She could be a soft pillow for all the boys care. Boys can't help it. Boys have to squirt or they go crazy, but you don't have to let them do it on your butt.

(Enter JUDY. TILLY hides her crying face.)

JUDY: Hi, Zoe. Hi, A-Hundred-and-Eighty-Eight-Pounds. What are you doing, Zoe? Where's your style? Roll up your sleeves—

ZOE: I forgot—

JUDY: Let me fix you—

ZOE: No, I don't have time now.

JUDY: I was going to fix you up at lunch, but I couldn't find you.

ZOE: I was in study room.

JUDY: I thought you were avoiding me. How come you didn't come over to Tilly's last night?

ZOE: ...My dad said no.

JUDY: We had a really good time. Sam called me.

TILLY: Sam my brother?

JUDY: Yeah. After I got home. He wants me to come over again.

ZOE: Yeah, I bet he can't wait.

JUDY: Yeah. He's going to invite some of his friends. Are you going to go?

ZOE: I didn't hear an invitation.

JUDY: Tilly wants us to. Don't you, Tilly?

(*No reply from* TILLY)

ZOE: Don't you have to go over to Rose's?

JUDY: I don't have to. I don't like Rose's mother. She's so stingy and they have more money than God. They could give a million dollars away and never even notice. That's where Rose gets her stinginess from. "Pay me back, pay me back." She is such a tightwad. You're not like that, are you, Zoe?

ZOE: No. I give away everything I have. And if I ever got more, I'm sure I'd give that away, too.

JUDY: Thanks.

TILLY: (*Angry*) What would *you* do, Judy? What would you do if you had a whole lot of money?

JUDY: I'd pay the rent for a year in advance. I don't know what I'd do with it if there was anything left after that.

TILLY: Would you give any to your friends?

JUDY: I said I don't know.

TILLY: You wouldn't. You'd keep it all to yourself and buy yourself naked butt clothes—

JUDY: What's with you, Tilly? Your family's doing okay. Nice house, plenty to eat, obviously. At least *your* father still pays child support.

(*Brief awkward pause*)

ZOE: Rose must have turned over a new leaf...one that isn't stingy...because I saw her a little while ago...she was in the hall...and she was giving people money.

JUDY: What?

ZOE: Yes, it was right after school, she was bringing ten-dollar bills out of her pocket and handing them to people.

JUDY: Where was she doing this?

ZOE: Everywhere. "Some for you, and some for you—." I heard her say, "Where's Judy?" She must be looking for you. To give you some.

JUDY: ...I better find her. See you later, Zoe. Come over to Tilly's. *(She exits.)*

ZOE: "Some for you...and some for you..."

TILLY: You are a terrible liar—

ZOE: Not that terrible— It got rid of her, didn't it?

TILLY: Rose is never going to give money to anybody.

ZOE: You're right about Judy. She does look like viruses and bacteria.

TILLY: Yeah. And that's what my mother wants me to be. I can't be like that. Why does she want me to be like that?

ZOE: I don't want you to be like that. I want you to be like you are. I want to be like you, too.

TILLY: Nobody wants to be like me.

ZOE: I do. You're not like anybody else, you don't look like anybody else—

TILLY: Yeah, nobody else is a big fat cow.

ZOE: I would give anything to be able to eat two cakes. *(Brief silence)* ...Do you want your cakes?

TILLY: ...You brought cakes?

(She begins to calm down.)

ZOE: Two cakes.

TILLY: Where are they?

ZOE: *(Gets them from under the bleachers)* I hid them this morning. They're kind of stale.

TILLY: I like stale cake.

ZOE: Then they're perfect.

TILLY: *(Opening a box)* You're not going to call me names, are you?

ZOE: I will never call you names. That's a white cake with berries and cream. It's my favorite.

TILLY: ...Do you need to get a piece?

ZOE: No. It's all for you. I got something else. A surprise. *(She slips under bleachers.)*

TILLY: *(Looks at cake.)* It's really pretty.

ZOE: *(Off)* There's a fork in there.

(TILLY sits down with the cake.)

TILLY: People should just let me eat. I don't worry when I eat. All the bad things go out of my mind. Everybody needs to send the bad things out of their mind—Mom smokes, Dad has a drink, Sam listens to his headphones and jerks off in the bathroom. So what if I need to eat something? Why is that so worst?

ZOE: *(Off)* Because those other things you can hide.

TILLY: Yeah. *(Eating)* Maybe I should try one of those hidden things—I could smoke. I could put razor cuts under my clothes like Judy.

(ZOE comes out from the bleachers. She is wearing a homemade fat suit designed to make her as fat as TILLY. It is inexpert. The fatness is extreme.)

ZOE: How is it?

TILLY: Delicious. *(Sees her, aghast)* ...What is that supposed to be? What are you doing?

ZOE: Imitation is the highest form of flattery. Just call me Garbage Belly Two.

TILLY: Take it off, take it off!

(Enter JUDY and ROSE.)

ROSE: Don't lie about me. Don't talk about me at all, ever.

TILLY: Oh, God—

ROSE: What are you wearing?!

JUDY: Rose wasn't giving away ten-dollar bills, Zoe.

ROSE: You are such a liar. Nobody can believe anything you say. Look at you, you're a freak.

ZOE: She must have given it all away. She even gave me some. *(She holds up a dollar.)* Look.

ROSE: That's not proof. That's lunch money from home.

ZOE: I get subsidized lunch. Ha.

JUDY: Where did she get the money, Rose?

ROSE: How should I know where she got it? It's a *dollar*—she found it on the ground—stole it out of her mother's purse. She didn't get it from me!

ZOE: My mother is dead, but if you want the money back so much, take it. Here.

ROSE: Stop it, stop pretending! Stop using me. *(To JUDY)* "Wait for me by the buses, Rose. Just wait 'til I get there. We'll go to the Fun Factory." You didn't come—you were never going to come—you just came when you thought there was money. Here, here, knock yourself out. *(She crinkles and throws bills.)* Greedy users. You're all pathetic.

JUDY: *(Picks up some bills)* I was coming—

ZOE: Dollars from her pocket, just like I said—

ROSE: Give me that, it's mine.

JUDY: I was picking it up for you—

ROSE: You think it's easy to have money? You try it.
Everybody wants it, everybody's got their hand out.
Am I supposed to give it all away? Who's going to take
care of me— You going to come to my house and bring
me food baskets when I'm poor again? You can get
poor again in a second. It can all go away in a second.
You can't just fritter...fritter it. You don't know the
money rules because you don't have any money!

JUDY: Well, you should teach them to us.

ROSE: Forget it. You weren't home last night, you
weren't there.

JUDY: I was doing homework.

ROSE: You were with them. And you don't even like
them, you're just sniffing around after her money. You
got all mine and now you're after hers.

JUDY: I'm trying to get a hundred dollars for your
mother.

ROSE: From her? You think she has a hundred dollars?
Look at her. What are you wearing? What is she
wearing? Is that some kind of heiress outfit? You're
a freak. You're both freaks. What's in the bakery box,
Fatty? Fat fattening things to make you fatter?

ZOE: Don't touch that box.

ROSE: (Over) Look at this. It's a whole fancy cake.

ZOE: It's for Tilly—

ROSE: Two cakes. Two huge cakes.

ZOE: She has cake needs.

ROSE: Not even Tilly can eat two cakes.

ZOE: *(Defending* TILLY*)* Yes, she can. Tilly defies the rules for volume and capacity.

ROSE: Because she's a big fat pig.

ZOE: *(Furious, shouts)* She is not a pig. She's a Garbage Belly!

TILLY: Shut up!

ZOE: And I'm a Garbage Belly, too. Compacting food right inside our stomachs, just like a big garbage truck. Can *you* do that?

TILLY: Shut up—shut up—

ROSE: I don't want to be able to do that. *(Relishing the concept)* Garbage Belly. Is that why you weigh a hundred and eighty-eight pounds? Because you're a Garbage Belly? You're a perfect trio. *(To* JUDY*)* I'm not going to play with you any more. I'm only going to play with my own kind—

JUDY: What did I do? I didn't do anything.

ROSE: Play with them. Three of a kind. A Freak, a Garbage Belly, and a User.

TILLY: ...I'd rather be Garbage Belly than a liar.

ROSE: Don't you call me a liar!

TILLY: Zoe. Zoe's the liar.

ZOE: Who? Why?!

ROSE: *(Over)* Yes, she is!

TILLY: She's a liar; she's a filthy liar. She lied about her inheritance. She—she made up that whole story about her great aunt. She is not an heiress, she is just a geek who hasn't got any money. She lied about it the whole time.

JUDY: There's no money?

ZOE: *(Playing Russians)* "Was not one lie..."

ROSE: You get a freak with no money, Judy.

TILLY: She did it to fool you. To watch you turn into money-grabbing users. To see how low you'd go—

JUDY: Are you going to get money or not?

ZOE: "Old auntie die."

JUDY: How much is it?

ZOE: "Many attorneys must settle vast estate."

ROSE: What's your dead aunt's name?

ZOE: "Sophie."

TILLY: That's her cat's name.

ZOE: "I name dead auntie after dead cat."

TILLY: Liar liar liar.

ZOE: "Not one lie. One good game."

JUDY: What a crummy cheat.

ROSE: A liar and a cheater.

(JUDY *starts to push, manhandle* ZOE. ZOE *struggles.*)

ZOE: "No manhandle important scientist!"

JUDY: Hold her, hold her.

ROSE: Here. Tie her hands up.

(ROSE *ties them with her scarf.* ZOE *retreats further into her game.*)

ZOE: "Oh no! Americans capture brilliant Russian scientist."

JUDY: I am always getting cheated.

ZOE: "Try make her reveal secrets."

ROSE: Insane, insane.

JUDY: Shut up, Zoe, shut up.

ROSE: Let's feed her to Garbage Belly.

ZOE: "They torture her until dawn."

JUDY: Hit her.

TILLY: You don't have to hit her. *(She takes out a handkerchief.)* She's more scared of the dark than punches even.

ZOE: *(Fear rising)* What...? What are you doing? Tilly— no— No, no, don't—

ROSE: Shut up. Shut up, stop biting me.

(ROSE covers ZOE's eyes with the handkerchief. ZOE becomes still, collapses.)

TILLY: *(Shouts at ZOE)* She's as scared as all the little children covered with tons and tons of terrorist rocks.

(ROSE releases her. Silence)

JUDY: What did you do to her?

ROSE: Me? You did it, too. Punch her. See if she moves.

JUDY: No. Come on, let's get out of here.

ROSE: I'm not going anywhere with you. You stay away from me. *(Exits)*

JUDY: *(Re ROSE)* What a bitch... *(Re ZOE)* She's alright, I can see her chest move. I'll see you later. I'm coming over to meet Sam's friends.

TILLY: Sure. Leave your panties at home, though. You can skip the freak dancing and they can all just stick it in you—in you—

JUDY: You are crazy—

TILLY: *(Over)* In you in you in you—my mother can watch, she'll love it.

JUDY: Out of your mind. Jeez— *(Exits)*

(TILLY pants, breathes, howls...exits.)

Scene 6

(Bleachers. Late afternoon. ZOE, *as she was.* TILLY *enters. Forced cheer)*

TILLY: I can't believe you're still here. Come on, game's over. What are you doing? How come you didn't get untied? You can get untied, it's not so tight. How come you didn't try to escape? Anybody can get out of a stupid scarf knot. *(Struggles with knot.)* ...I guess it is kind of tight. Rose made it too tight. What a bitch. Your father's in a state. The taxi guy went over to the bakery when you didn't show up. Everybody's looking for you—the teachers and the people from the community college. I saw the fat kid. You're right, he is fatter than me. They went all through the school. I thought they'd find you, but then Rose the bitch said she'd already looked here, so nobody else did. The police won't call you a missing person until tomorrow, so your Dad is offering a reward. *(She pulls on the knot with her teeth.)* Okay, I got it. Know what Sam said, he said you were probably raped and murdered—he said I was lucky. Nobody would ever want to rape and murder me, I'm too fat. I hope Sam and his friends rape and murder Judy and go to prison for life and get raped and murdered there. Shit.

(Untied, ZOE *collapses.)*

TILLY: Take your blindfold off. Come on, quit fooling around. *(Brief pause)* Okay, maybe I shouldn't have helped them, but you shouldn't have called me Garbage Belly, that was a secret and you just shouted it out in the world. What was I supposed to think, you screaming Garbage Belly with them around? They're going to tell everybody— Everybody in school is going to call me that. I have to run away from home.

*(*TILLY *takes off the blindfold.* ZOE *is in a daze, eyes unfocused.)*

TILLY: What's wrong with your eyes?

(TILLY *leans* ZOE *against the bleachers. The stirring of fear*)

TILLY: Okay, you can tell on me. I'll go with you, I'll tell on myself.
You don't know how I felt. If I had a gun I would've shot you. I'd have shot you all. I deserve some bad punishment. You can say what it is. You can be the one who thinks it up, okay?
Okay?
Come on, wake up. We got to—we got to get to your Dad. He cried in front of everybody. We got to get there and tell him you're okay.
Please wake up.
(*Increasing panic and sadness*)
Zoe...please, please talk to me. You're the only person who was ever nice to me—you're the only person I have—please come back into your mind. Please don't leave me. Don't leave me all alone. What am I going to do? What am I going to do without you? I'll die without you—I love you Zoe, please wake up, please, please...
(*She picks up umbrella, Russian accent.*)
"Oh, I so sad I not see my good friend *Yelena*. Natasha need her good friend Yelena to help hide valuable umbrella—valuable magic shield. Only Yelena think up good hiding place for magic shield."
(*No response. Frantic, desperate, she sings.*)
Rock-a-bye baby in the tree top, when the wind blows the cradle will rock. When the bow breaks, the cradle will fall, and down will come Zoe...

ZOE: Mommy...

TILLY: Oh, Zoe, come back to me, please come back to me.

ZOE: Tilly?

TILLY: I'll never let you be in the dark, never.

ZOE: Tilly. My Tilly.

TILLY: Please don't hate me.

ZOE: Tilly—

TILLY: You're my only person...my only one.

ZOE: *(Amazed)* I fell into a well.

TILLY: I made it dark. I put you in the dark.

ZOE: I couldn't move.

TILLY: You're okay now.

ZOE: It was so dark.

TILLY: Oh, I'm so sorry—I'm sorry—

ZOE: I couldn't reach my matches.

TILLY: Here, here, I got some.

ZOE: I wanted to die to stop being afraid.

TILLY: Do you hate me?

ZOE: I don't think so.

TILLY: We can play Russians—Russians and dead rich aunt.

ZOE: ...And Garbage Belly?

TILLY: Anything you want.

ZOE: *(She looks at herself in the fat suit.)* Look. I'm just like you, just like you.

(TILLY *lights a match. They watch it.*)

END OF PLAY

www.ingramcontent.com/pod-product-compliance
Lightning Source LLC
Chambersburg PA
CBHW052220090426
42741CB00010B/2616